Accounting

───── ❧❦❧ ─────

Accounting made simple, basic accounting principles, and how to do your own bookkeeping

Table of Contents

Introduction 1

Chapter 1 Ten Bookkeeping Basics 3

Chapter 2 Reading and Creating a P/L Statement 7

Chapter 3 How to Read and Create a Balance Sheet 12

Chapter 4 Paying Taxes to the Government 22

Chapter 5 Sales Tax 28

Chapter 6 How to Create a Cash Flow Statement................. 32

Chapter 7 How to Budget Your Business Finances............... 35

Chapter 8 Tips to Keep on Track with Accounting 40

Chapter 9 Financial Ratios...................................... 45

Chapter 10 Stockholder's Equity 52

Chapter 11 Cash VS. Accrual.................................... 54

Chapter 12 Depreciation.. 57

Chapter 13 Inventory Accounting 60

Chapter 14 Definitions of Accounting Terms................. 63

Conclusion 67

Introduction

—————— ✣✣✣✣ ——————

Thank you for taking the time to pick up this book about Accounting!

This book covers the topic of accounting basics and will teach you all you need to know to understand small business accounting!

For small business owners, accounting can often be an extremely daunting task, and something that gets neglected. However, keeping accurate accounting records and knowing your numbers well is absolutely vital in running a successful business!

This book will teach you all of the accounting basics you need to know, in a simple, no-nonsense manner that will have you understanding your accounting with ease! You will learn all about different statements, budgets, taxes, and how to manage and understand all of them from an accounting standpoint.

Basic accounting principles and practices will be explained in detail. Everything you need to do on a day-to-day basis is covered here in-depth. Also, some more advanced topics will be briefly explained, so that you have some idea of how to handle them should they arise or need to be addressed. This book's aim is not to turn you into a qualified accountant – but rather to prepare you for managing and understanding small business accounting, so that you can competently and confidently manage your own books.

At the completion of this book you will have a good understanding of accounting, will be able to manage your own books, and be well on your way to running a successful business!

Once again, thanks for taking the time to read this book, I hope you find it to be helpful and informative!

Chapter 1

------ ❧❧❧❧❧ ------

Ten Bookkeeping Basics

Congratulations on getting your new business started! Now that you are up and running, it is time to take a look at some accounting basics. There are far more than ten, but the ones we are going to look at in this chapter are the most common ones used with small businesses. If you are not able or wanting to hire an accountant or a bookkeeper, these ten basics are going to be a lifesaver. Once we have covered these ten basics, we will go into a little more depth and discuss taxes, budgets, P/L statements, balance sheets, cash flow and sales tax. This will be all you will need to start handling the day to day accounting that comes along with small business ownership.

Cash. Really, this is about as basic as it gets. Any of your transactions will go through your cash account. This is so vital that many accountants will often use two journals. There is one for cash disbursements and another for cash receipts. Keeping these two separate from the get go will make life that much simpler.

Accounts Receivable. Receivables are transactions in which a product has been sold, but the money isn't collected immediately and these are very important to track. This is money that customers owe you, so keeping it up to date is crucial. Depending on the size of the transaction, you can set up 30, 45 or 90-day invoice turnaround requirements with your customer. 30 days is standard and the sooner you get paid for your product, the less you will have to worry about collecting the money at a later date.

Inventory. This is product you have in stock and is compared to having money sitting on the shelf. Obviously, this will need to be carefully tracked and accounted for. The size of your inventory will probably determine how often you do a full inventory count. Again, the standard for this tends to be right around every thirty days. To keep close track of your inventory, physical counts of what is on hand is something you should get in the habit of completing immediately.

Accounts Payable. Ah, the dreaded accounts payable or for short, A/P. Unfortunately, business isn't all about receivables. As an owner, you will most likely have to pay for utilities, space rental, equipment rental, and for employees, and that's just to name a few things that payables will cover. Each business will be different and you'll know what needs to be paid and when by keeping close track of your payables. This will ensure you are paying your bills in a timely fashion and that you don't make the mistake of paying someone twice. In small business, sometimes there are discounts if you pay your bills early. Check with all of your creditors to see if this is an option. If so, it is a great way to save money! And, as always, it can't hurt to ask.

Loans Payable. This is accounting for loans you may have taken out on equipment, a building, furniture, vehicles or anything else you needed to start your business. This is also crucial as it keeps you abreast as to what the balances are and what loans are due when.

Sales. This account is where you will keep track of the revenue from what is sold. Always record sales in a timely manner as this point is critical for knowing exactly where you are at with the money coming in from sales.

Purchases. This is the account that will track materials or goods you purchased for your business. This is a major component because you will deduct this from your sales to determine your small business gross profit.

Payroll Expenses. This tends to be the biggest cost for most companies. Unless it is just you and one or two other people, this piece is probably going to be the most time consuming. Honestly, even if your company is small, or it is just you being paid for the time being, there is a lot to know about all the different payroll expenses. Payroll comes with taxes, workman's comp insurance and many other components that the government requires businesses to keep track of and accurately report. Each state will vary slightly as to what is required as part of the payroll expenses. Just make sure to check with your local authority before writing that first payroll check.

Owners' Equity. This component keeps track of how much each owner has put into the business. If it's just you, awesome! There isn't as much to keep track of. Money put into the business should be tracked by *capital* accounts and money withdrawn will appear in *drawing* accounts. This is so all business owners can see exactly what is going on with cash flow, what is coming in and what is going out.

Retained Earnings. This account will keep track of profits that have been reinvested in the business, but are not paid back to the owners. These are cumulative, and means they will appear in your running total of money that was started upon opening the company. This is one of the easiest accounts to maintain and it is important to those in the company who wish to track how well the company performs over time.

Although many business owners consider accounting a tedious task, it really is a crucial part of running your business. Understanding the basics will make it less of a chore and will aid in running the business much more effectively.

There is a lot to accounting. However, the ten basics we covered in this chapter are foundational and will be what you need to start keeping your own books. At a later date, if the budget allows, perhaps you will be able to hire a professional to handle your books for you. Until then, these fundamentals will get you on the right path to small business accounting.

Chapter 2

------ ✥❧✥❧ ------

Reading and Creating a P/L Statement

P/L is an abbreviation for the Profit and Loss statement. This statement is a snapshot of the company's finances for a period of time. Generally, it can be over the course of a year, a quarter or a month. These statements are pretty simple to read and depending on what kind of record you keep (electronic or paper), there are free, downloadable forms on the internet. Should you choose to keep paper files, you can download them online and print them out. Most office stores will also carry these.

Most small business owners have started a business because they are passionate about the product they sell or the services they provide. The main headache with business ownership tends to be accounting. It is all about numbers, tracking things, paying bills and taxes...it does seem daunting, but is an essential part of running a successful business. Believe it or not, there are hundreds of entrepreneurs who never looked at their profit/loss statement simply because they couldn't understand them. That can be detrimental to your business' success and while this book can't teach you to be a CPA (Certified Public Accountant), it can help you learn the fundamentals of accounting so that your business can succeed and grow.

The formula for your P/L statement is pretty basic. It is essentially your sales minus your cost equals your profit. Everything else in relation to the business cash flow and payables is a matter of breaking out your sales and costs into more detail and adding in the subtotals. Your total sales are most often shown at the top of the P/L statement. Costs are shown directly below the sales and the overall profit is shown at the bottom. There may be several subtotals as you go down the sheet or column, but the formula for P/L remains the same. It is sales minus cost equals profit.

Unfortunately, the terms used for sales, profit and loss can vary and will often make accounting seem more difficult than it needs to be. As an example, sales is usually referred to as income or revenue. Costs are also called expenses while profits will be named income. Along the same lines, the P/L statement itself can be referred to as a ledger or income statement. All of these can be confusing, but don't worry too much about the terminology.

The sales for your business may be broken down into several components. An example of this can be that perhaps your sheet breaks out material costs, labor and overhead into separate categories. There are literally an infinite number of ways for costs to be broken out, but once you get to the total sales, everything else is simply a cost broken down and out one way or another.

As mentioned, there are several ways to subdivide costs, but the most useful way is to subdivide them into costs that are most closely related to the delivery of your service or product and those that aren't. An example of this is a company that manufactures and sells several types of widgets. Their P/L would be broken down by the cost of the components they use to create the different kinds of widgets, the cost of labor, or the people who make the widgets along with machines assembling them as well as the cost of the facility in which the widgets are produced. These types of costs are called cost of goods sold (COGS) because they are directly related to the making of the company's widgets.

Now that we've provided an example for a business with a product, we'll discuss what a service based businesses will experience.

In the service business, the term used is COS or cost of service. An example of this is a lawn mowing company that would need to include the cost of the employees completing the work as well as the cost of fuel and other supplies needed to perform day to day tasks for the service.

Sales minus the COGS is known as the gross profit, which is money the company earns after the cost of delivering the service or product has been deducted. It also includes the money necessary to cover other costs related to running the business, yet still generating a profit.

Other costs for your business will not be associated with the cost of producing the widgets. Those types of cost might include the people who sell the widgets (salesforce), office staff or perhaps the president's compensation. These costs are usually referred to as SGA, which is Selling and General Administrative costs. When this is added, the P/L is broken down into two parts. Your gross profit minus your SGA will equal profit and sales minus your COGS will equal the gross profit. Below you will see a general example of a P/L statement or ledger.

Revenue	**1 000**
-/- COGS	-550
Direct sales cost	-20
Depreciation	-45
Gross profit	**385**
as % of sales	*38,5%*
R&D expense	-10
Sales & admin expense	-15
Other salaries	-15
Other office costs	-5
Total OPEX	**-45**
as % of sales	*-4,5%*
Financial costs/gains	10
Extraordinary cost/gains	-15
EBIT	**335**
as % of sales	*33,5%*
add back depr	45
EBITDA	**380**
Interest cost	-7
Company income tax	-90
Net Income	**238**
as % of sales	*23,8%*

In this chapter, we talked about the P/L statement and how to read it. Because we have covered so much, let's recap all of this information in its simplest terms.

At the top of your P/L statement is the gross revenue or sale of merchandise/goods that directly relate to your company's primary operation. This gross revenue does *not* include any deductions yet. Returns deducted from the gross revenue will give you the net revenue. From the net revenue, you'll deduct the cost of your raw materials that were used to create goods for your sales. That will give you your gross margin or gross profit. We consider this *gross* because your other expenses are not yet accounted for in the overall figures.

Next, you'll deduct the general expenses for operating the company which will include, rent, utilities, employee payroll, administrative expenses, freight, depreciation and amortization. The total from this will give you the net operating income that is representative of the total revenue that is left over after you've accounted for all of the costs of simply doing business.

Finally, the P/L statement needs to account for interest accrued, interest paid on borrowed funds (loans), or any income from outside investments. All of these can be listed as their own line item or combined onto one line. This will give you profit before tax. After that, the burden of tax for the period (year, quarter or month), is deducted. That total will bring you to the bottom line or your net profit.

As you saw in the example provided in this chapter, a P/L statement can be expressed in % figures, but can also be presented with simple dollar amounts instead. Both formats are definitely useful in helping you to better understand the economics of your business.

Chapter 3

–––––– ❦❦❦ ––––––

How to Read and Create a Balance Sheet

The balance sheet, which is also known as a statement of the company's financial position, will show the company assets, its liabilities and the owners net worth or equity. The balance sheet combined with the cash flow statement and the income statement are the basis and foundation of your company's financial statements. This is one of those statements that, as a business owner, it is important you understand how to read it, analyze it and what it means. This chapter will focus on how to create and read your company's balance sheet.

There are several platforms for you to use to create your own balance sheet. This can be done in excel, Quickbooks or templates can be downloaded from a variety of sources online.

First, we will go into detail as to how the balance sheet works so that you can gain a deeper understanding of it. Basically, it is separated into two parts that will ultimately work together and give you a clear sight into your company's financial status. The equation necessary to make this work is assets equal liabilities plus shareholders' equity. Both parts of this balance sheet must either be equal to one another or balance one another out. The basic formula means that the assets (or the means used to operate the company) are going to be balanced by the company's financial obligations combined with the equity of investments that are brought into the company in addition to its retained earnings.

Now, assets are what the company uses for the operation of the business whereas equity and liabilities are the main two sources that will support the assets. The owner or shareholder equity is the amount of money that's invested in the company as well as the retained earnings, which is what shows a true representation of what source is funding the business.

At this juncture, it is important to state that the balance sheet is a snapshot of the company's overall financial position at one point (one month, for instance) or at a specific place in time.

ASSETS

In order to properly read your balance sheet, you'll need to understand the types of assets that are figured into the balance sheet. There are only two types of assets that the balance sheet will require to properly account for the business' financial position. The two types are current and non-current assets. We will discuss them both so you have a good understanding of what the difference is between the two and why both are important to have on your balance sheet.

Current Assets

Current assets include accounts receivable, cash or cash equivalents, and inventory. In general, the current assets only have a lifespan of a year, maybe less, because they are converted into cash easily. Speaking of cash, it is the most fundamental part of your current assets. Cash can also include any non-restricted bank accounts you have, as well as checks. Cash and their equivalents are the safest assets that are ready to be converted into cash at any given point. Accounts receivables are the short-term monies due to the company by the clients. Because most companies will sell product to their clients on a credit type basis, they will be held in the current assets until the client pays them off.

The final type of current assets for the balance sheet includes your raw materials, any goods that are currently in progress and those that are in the finished stage, waiting to be sold to your customer. Depending on how your company is set up and how it functions, your inventory will differ from others. A good example is this; manufacturing firms tend to carry large amounts of raw materials and keep them in inventory for their product, whereas a retail company will not have raw materials. The retailer will have products previously purchased from a manufacturer, but their product is already on the shelves for retail sale.

Non-Current Assets

Next, we have the non-current assets. They are assets that cannot be easily turned into cash and/or consist of a lifespan that will be a year or more. Non-current assets are also referred to as tangible assets which consists of computers, buildings, land and machinery. However, non-current assets can also include intangible assets, which are things like patents, copyrights and goodwill. The intangible assets are not considered physical objects, but are often a resource that can either make or break the company. An example of this is the brand name, which is something that should never be underestimated.

Depreciation will be calculated and then deducted from most of the above listed assets, which is a representation of the economic costs of the asset over the duration of its life.

LIABILITIES

Before we take a look at a balance sheet, let's briefly talk about the different types of liabilities and shareholder's equities, both of which are part of the balance sheet.

The liabilities are what are on the opposite side of your balance sheet and they include financial obligations your company owes to parties not affiliated with your business. As with assets, liabilities can be either current or long-term. The long-term liabilities include debts that are due at least a year out from the balance sheet. The current liabilities are those that must be paid or will be due within one year. These can include accounts payable or other short-term loans. It can also include long-term borrowings, which are things like the latest payment of interest on a ten-year loan.

The shareholder's equity is the money that was initially invested in the business during its startup phase. At the end of each fiscal year, a company can decide whether or not it will reinvest its net earnings (after taxes) into the company. Those are considered retained earnings and they are transferred from your income statement to your balance sheet then into the account of the shareholder. That account is what represents the company's net worth. For the balance sheet to properly balance, the total assets on one side must equal the shareholder's equity plus the total liabilities on the other side.

Now that we've talked about the formulas needed for the balance sheet, let's look at what a balance sheet looks like. There is a simple example for a fictitious business on the following page.

Paul's Guitar Shop, Inc. Balance Sheet December 31, 2015					
Assets			**Liabilities**		
Current Assets			Current Liabilities		
Cash		32,800	Accounts Payable		49,000
Accounts Receivable		300	Accrued Expenses		450
Prepaid Rent		1,000	Unearned Revenue		1,000
Inventory		39,800	Total Current Liabilities		50,450
			Long-term Liabilities		99,500
Total Current Assets		73,900	**Total Liabilities**		149,950
			Owner's Equity		
Long-term Assets			Owner's Equity		
Leasehold Improvements	100,000		Retained Earnings		11,950
Accumulated Depreciation	(2,000)	98,000	Common Stock		10,000
Total Long-term Assets		98,000	Total Owner's Equity		21,950
Total Assets:		171,900	**Total Liabilities and Owner's Equity**		171,900

Understanding Your Balance Sheet

When you look at this example of a balance sheet, you will see that it is broken down into two areas. The assets are shown on the left while the liabilities and shareholders equity are shown on the right. This is a great example of a balance sheet because it is quite clear the sheet is *in balance*. It is also organized well. The liabilities and assets section is organized by how current each account is. As far as assets are concerned, the accounts are categorized by most liquid to least. Where the liabilities are concerned, those accounts are organized by short-term to long-term borrowings as well as other obligations.

Balance sheets can also be presented with the assets on the top half of a page, and the liabilities on the bottom half.

Now that we have seen an example of a balance sheet and have a better understanding of the components that go into it, we can look at some of the different ways to analyze the information that is on the sheet. The most common way to do this is by using the information provided by financial ratios. Financial ratios will also be covered in more depth in a later chapter.

The financial ratio analysis consists of formulas used to gather insight into the operations of the company and the company itself. When using financial ratios for the balance sheet, you will get a better idea as to the financial condition of the company as well as the operational efficiency. Please note that some of the ratios also require information from multiple financial statements, which can include the income statement and balance sheet.

There are two main, yet slightly different kinds of ratios that will utilize information from the balance sheet. These are your activity ratios and your financial strength ratios. In particular, the financial strength ratios like the debt to equity ratios and the working capital will give information on how obligations can be leveraged and how well the company is able to balance and meet said obligations.

These ratios will give your investors an idea as to how financially secure the company is and how well the company is able to finance itself. Activity ratios will mainly focus on the current accounts, which will show how well the company is able to manage the operating cycle. The operating cycle includes inventory, payables and receivables. The ratios will all provide valuable insight into the company's overall operational efficiency.

The bottom line is that the balance sheet, along with your cash flow and income statements are decisive tools for your company's success. It also gives future investors (or those currently invested) insight into your company and its overall ability to operate. The balance sheet is a glimpse into your company's accounts at any specific point in time. It covers the assets, shareholder's equity, and liabilities of the company. This sheet is important and its purpose is to give the user an idea of what kind of financial position that the company is in as well as an idea as to what the company owes and owns.

Creating Your Own Balance Sheet

We've talked a lot about what goes into a balance sheet, seen an example of one, and now it's time to look at ways you can create your very own one for your business.

As we mentioned at the start of this chapter, there are many platforms you can use to create your balance sheet. If you are proficient with excel, that's a great tool to use because there are functions that will sum columns automatically, making the likelihood of a mathematical error smaller. If you are operating your own small business, chances are you are already using a program like Quickbooks to perform the daily accounting functions. Quickbooks does have a balance sheet function and if you've already purchased the program, you might as well get the most out of your money and use that function.

No matter the platform you use, there are key components you will need in your balance sheet, which we will detail below. In general, Quickbooks will have a balance sheet as part of its software, at which point you'll only need to put the proper headings onto the sheet. If you are creating one yourself, here are the steps:

1. **Title and a heading**. The most common used title is *balance sheet*. However, you can also use something like, *Statement of Financial Position*. The heading needs to include your company's legal name and the dates of representation. For example, December 31, 2015. This would cover the entire year up to that point and the balance sheet for that previous year is usually created at the start of the new year. Don't wait too long, however. Keeping accurate, up to date records is important.

2. **Format**. There are two ways you can format your balance sheet. In the accounting form, assets will be listed on the left side and totaled to equal your sum of the liabilities and the shareholder's equity, which will go on the right side. You can also use the report form. This is a running format where the assets will be shown at the top of the page immediately followed by the stockholder's equity and liabilities. On occasion, the total liabilities will be deducted from the total assets so that it will equal the shareholder's equity.

3. **Captions**. These include headings in the balance sheet that are designed to designate the major accounts by group that need to be totaled or subtotaled. In this category, your balance sheet must include three primary captions: liabilities, assets and shareholder's equity.

4. **Order and presentation of captions**. Here, you will want to start with the items usually held for conversion to cash, and then rank them in order according to the expected speed of conversion, also known as liquidity. After that, you'll follow with the items that are primarily used for operations, but can also be converted into cash. Here, you will also rank those into liquidity order. Finally, you'll finish with costs that can be deferred to future periods and cannot be converted into cash. Below, you'll see an example of how to set up your balance sheet according to the above listed guidelines.

Cash

- Inventories

- Intangible assets

- Deferred charges

- Marketable securities (short-term)

- Equipment and property

- Investments (long-term)

- Accounts receivables and trade notes

Liabilities

- Debt (long-term)

- Demand notes

- Accrued expenses

- Trade accounts payable

- Any other long-term liabilities

Components of Stockholder's Equity

- Common stock

- Preferred stock

- Retained earnings

- Additional paid in capital

- Treasury stock

- Other accumulated or comprehensive income

In this chapter, we have seen what kind of details need to go into a balance sheet, an example of a balance sheet, and the platforms you can use to create your own balance sheet. When deciding to make your own, be sure to use all of the information contained in this chapter as well as the items outlined above. Keeping a current and detailed record within the balance sheet is a major key to ensuring the success of your company.

Chapter 4

─ ─ ─ ─ ─ ❧❧❧❧ ─ ─ ─ ─ ─

Paying Taxes to the Government

As an employee, you probably didn't know too much about how taxes were transmitted from your employer to the government. Now, as a small business owner, that will be part of your responsibilities. In addition to paying federal and state taxes, small business owners must match social security and Medicare taxes. We will discuss the tax requirements that you, the small business owner, will be responsible for.

Estimated Tax

First, there are the estimated tax payments. This is the money you'll set aside when you are paid from clients. When you were an employee, this was automatically deducted from your check. Now, as the owner, you will want to make sure you set aside enough estimated tax to cover what you will actually be liable for when it comes time to file your taxes. A general rule is; if you are expected to owe at least one-thousand dollars in taxes for that year after subtracting all of your tax credits, it would be wise to make estimated tax payments. This will do wonders for your bottom line. If, at the end of the year, you've not made estimated tax payments, you can expect to owe a rather large sum of money to the IRS. Likewise, if you estimate properly, you may not owe any money, or the amount you do owe will be much more manageable. I cannot stress enough how important it is to make your estimated tax payments. It will lessen your financial burden and tax related stress.

If your earnings from the year prior to opening your business are going to be less than or close to what you think you are going to earn in the first year of running your business, paying the full one-hundred percent of what you paid in the previous year for taxes is definitely the way to go. In all honesty, this is the easiest method and formula to use when it comes to paying estimated taxes. If you believe that your earnings while you were an employee were markedly higher than you expect in your first year of business, one-hundred percent of the previous year's taxes will likely be too burdensome. If this is the case, there is another method you can use to estimate your taxes.

Basically, you will need to plan on paying ninety-percent of what you will end up owing for the entire year. Remember, we mentioned how important it is to make those estimated tax payments to lessen your burden at the end of the year. The 90/10 ratio may sound reasonable, but if your business is wildly successful, ten-percent can turn out to be quite a lot of money. Make sure you keep up with your tax payments each quarter.

Calculating exactly how much you'll need to pay to the IRS every quarter can be difficult. However, the IRS website has a form you can download, which is great. The IRS doesn't expect you to know how to do this, especially if this is your first year in business. The form you'll need to download is part of the 1040 ES, which is the estimated tax for individuals. This will calculate how much tax you are likely to have for the year.

They base this off of your quarterly income so if one quarter you don't perform as well, that's okay. Your taxes won't be the same, which will be less of a burden to you. At the end of each quarter, go through the worksheet and complete your estimated tax liability. It'll give you a total, which is what you'll need to send to the IRS.

As we've mentioned, you'll need to submit your taxes to the IRS four times per year, or at the end of each quarter. It is always an option for you to make your tax payments electronically through the *Electronic Federal Tax Payment System*. The IRS expects payments to be made by January 15, April 15, June 15 and September 15. One issue you might have is the first payment of the year on January 15th. If you did really well in the last quarter of the year, your tax burden will be higher. It sounds daunting, but if you remember to send your payments in each quarter, it is much easier on your overall financials to do that as opposed to once per year on the fifteenth. Also, this will get easier to estimate as time goes on. The first few years in business can be rough with all the learning curves. Soon, paying those estimated taxes will be a breeze.

One final tip on the subject of estimated taxes. If financially possible, try to keep a pretty decent sum of money set aside for your taxes just in case you wind up owing more than you anticipated.

Self-Employment Tax

The next type of tax we are going to cover is the self-employment tax. To be clear, there isn't actually a self-employment tax imposed by the government. This refers specifically to Medicare and social security tax payments. When you were an employee, about 6.2% of your earnings went to social security while approximately 1.65% went to Medicare tax. The employer you formerly worked for was responsible for matching those tax amounts. Now, as the employer and small business owner, it is your responsibility to match the amounts listed above. The formula for this is: you will pay 15.3% in Medicare and social security taxes on 92.35 of your net earnings. While the portion you must match is tax deductible, it doesn't provide much of a cushion for the blow and only drops your overall responsibility on the self-employment tax by a couple of percentage points.

The self-employment tax is not one that will be paid quarterly, either. This is turned into the government annually in one lump sum using the aforementioned IRS form schedule SE for self-employment taxes. As this tax is required yearly, on April 15th, it is a good idea to be prepared and have a significant amount of money as a cushion for when this tax is due. Since you are in your first year of business, it will be difficult to properly estimate this tax and it is a good idea to be as prepared as you possibly can be.

Payroll Tax

Next, are payroll taxes. Even if in your first year you can only afford to hire one employee, you will have to pay payroll taxes. Along those same lines, if your business is structured as a C Corporation, you will be considered an employee and even if it is just you, that requires a payroll tax. Depending on the state you live in, you'll also probably be required to pay a state unemployment tax as well as the worker's compensation fund. The intricacies of payroll taxes could require an entire book of their own, and will vary from location to location. Simply make sure that you are allowing for these taxes when calculating the amount of money you will be paying to your employees.

Tax Deductions

Finally, we are going to lighten things up a bit and talk about tax deductions! This is one of many perks of owning a small business. The deductions are where you subtract business expenses from taxable income. In general, this includes office furniture, computers, office supplies and sometimes health insurance can be part of your tax deductions every year.

It is important to note that you should not simply begin buying unnecessary things for your business just because they may be tax deductible. The tax deduction is meant to help lessen the burden and provide you with a credit at the end of the year. It is not free money. Tax credits don't equal money in your pocket. It simply makes what you owe the IRS a little less. Some of the most important tax deductions include; meals and entertainment for customers, phone, internet, health insurance premiums, loan interest, vehicle use, self-employed retirement plan contributions, or traveling for business to name a few.

Business Type

We've covered quite a bit in the way of taxes, but let's touch briefly on the formation of your business and how it affects your tax liability. When you are preparing to form your business, there is a form you will fill out that defines what type of business you plan on running. The types of business include; partnership, limited liability corporation (LLC), sole proprietorship, or a C corporation. Each has its own tax liability guidelines and you'll want to know which type of business will be both best suited to your needs and your future growth, as well as what your general tax liability will be based on the type of business you operate.

Remember, taxes in general can be intimidating. However, the IRS is pretty good about working with small businesses, especially those in their first year. They do not expect you to be efficient, and they understand that mistakes will be made. There is nothing to fear when completing your taxes and working with the IRS so long as you keep accurate records each quarter and throughout the year.

Chapter 5

---- ❧❧❧ ----

Sales Tax

I bet you thought the dreaded "T" word (taxes) was something we were done discussing, right? Sorry to say, that is not the case. In addition to paying taxes to the federal government, any business that sells goods to a consumer is subject to a sales tax. Sales taxes are regulated both at the state level and local levels. This is something specific to where you live, which we will get into in this chapter. Some cities and counties don't have sales tax, but those are few and far between. Some counties or cities also have a lower sales tax than others depending on how rural the town or county is. Finally, there are actually six states in which sales tax does not apply at the state level and they are; Montana, Delaware, Alaska, New Hampshire, Hawaii and Oregon.

First, let's talk about what exactly sales tax is. It is defined as a tax imposed by the state, that is paid by the consumer at the retail point of purchase. This sales tax can be imposed for goods or services. The small business owner is responsible for and are required to assess the sales tax, collect it from the consumer, then turn around and pay it to the appropriate agency within a designated amount of time. This varies from state to state and is something you'll want to look into for your specific state. Also, if you have retail locations in other states, you'll want to familiarize yourself with the legalities and sales tax requirements for each county, city, and state in which you operate.

It is important to state that in order for your company to legally collect sales taxes, you must obtain a sales tax permit. The Small Business Association (SBA) has links on their website to find the specific requirements and forms for each state, making it easy for you to find what you need, as well as details on how to file your permit with your state.

Like your federal taxes, you'll want to file your sales taxes quarterly, or even monthly. As we discussed in the previous chapter, keeping on top of your tax liability whether it is federal or sales taxes will lessen your burden when it comes time to file your yearly taxes on April 15th. The sales tax has its own, special return and on it you will report taxable sales, report all sales, exempt sales and amount of taxes due. Sales taxes accrued and not paid on time will result in serious penalties. Make sure you check what the specific requirements for your state are, as it will vary.

There are items or goods that are exempt from sales tax. Again, you'll want to check with your local government to clarify, but in general there are three transactions in which you are not required to collect a sales tax.

1. Resold Items. Resellers and retailers don't usually pay sales tax on wholesale purchases. In the instance of wholesale, there is the assumption that the consumer purchasing the items at the point of purchase will pay the sales tax.

2. Non-profits. Any sale made to a non-profit organization will, in general, be exempt from sales tax.

3. Raw Materials. This is specific to companies that sell and produce items that are raw materials for other goods. Those items tend to be exempt from sales taxes.

If you sell to customers in other states, you are probably wondering how sales tax works. What if you are selling to a customer in a state where they are exempt from sales tax? Whether you are selling online or to a customer who perhaps calls in an order and you are shipping out of state, the sales tax can get tricky and there are some gray areas.

Here is a common scenario. Your bricks and mortar building is in California and you have a customer from Utah ordering some of your product. This is the gray area we mentioned a moment ago. If you do not have a bricks and mortar building in the state where the customer is ordering from and the product will go, you are not required to collect a sales tax. If your home base is in California, but you also have a building in Utah where the customer is also located, you absolutely must collect sales tax in ordinance with Utah's sales tax laws.

In the instance your customer is ordering from your online store, and they are not tax exempt nor do they live in a state that has no sales tax, you will need to determine the proper tax rate. This can be where things get a little tricky, but Google and the IRS website have all the information you need in determining what the appropriate sales tax would be for your out of state customer. It is prudent to mention that if you plan on selling products online, it would be worthwhile to invest in an online shopping cart software. These programs will automatically calculate the sales tax for the customer purchasing your product based on the state they live in.

Tax in general can be tricky, but sales tax especially, because there are thousands of different tax jurisdictions all across the United States. It is next to impossible to attempt to commit them all to memory. Use the resources you have available to you to ease the sense of feeling overwhelmed when it comes to sales tax calculations for all fifty states. There is no need to concern yourself with knowing them all. That would be far too much for you to remember. Keep excellent records of the sales taxes on each transaction. If you are doing business in just one state, it will be simple. However, if you are selling online to all fifty states, try to find a way to keep an accurate record of taxes. Separating by state is one of the easiest methods. There is no need to break it out into city and county.

Chapter 6

------ ❧❧❧ ------

How to Create a Cash Flow Statement

Capturing the cash flow picture is not always easy. However, it is important to get an accurate snapshot so you can monitor trends with your cash and keep your business records up to date and accurate. Cash flow budgets and statements are one of the things you'll want to keep track of on a quarterly basis. This is one of the statements you can also keep once per month if it makes it easier for you to track.

The cash flow statement is one of the main financial statements your company will use. It goes along with your income statement, balance sheet and the statement for stockholder's equity. The purpose of your cash flow statement is to report cash generated and disbursed or used during any specific time frame. As mentioned earlier, it could be monthly or quarterly. Going out much further than that might pose problems in the future.

There are four categories that the cash flow statement will organize and they are:

1. Investing activities. Under this heading, the statement will report purchases and sales of plant and equipment, property and long-term investments.

2. Financing activities. This portion of the report will show issuance and repurchase of the company's stocks and bonds as well as the repayment of dividends.

3. Operating activities. This category will convert items that are reported on your income statement from accruing accounting to cash.

4. Supplemental information. Under this heading, you will see the exchange of items that did not involve cash. You will also see interest and income tax paid here.

Now that we've broken down the ways in which your cash flow statement will be organized, we can talk about the two different methods of creating a cash flow statement.

The first is the **direct method.** This method will track specific outflow and inflow from the activities of operating. In its basest explanation; this method subtracts money spent from money received.

The second method is the **indirect method.** We are only mentioning it because there are two, but the indirect method is by far the most difficult. It begins with the net income of your business and then factors in depreciation.

The direct method is recommended unless you are already an accountant and you understand and prefer the indirect method.

When it comes to creating the cash flow statement, there are several methods you can use. You can create one manually and in this method, you'll review income and expenses based on the four categories listed above. You can also use a spreadsheet you create on your own. Excel is a good place to create spreadsheets as it can calculate data for you with the sum function. You can also find free cash flow statements online or at office stores. Finally, you can also use Quickbooks. The functionality of that program for all accounting purposes serves the needs of most small businesses, and it isn't overly expensive to purchase. Don't forget that software could be one of those tax write offs, so it might be wise to invest in the program. No matter the method you choose, remember your entries need to show your cash brought in and paid out each month over the course of the cash flow statement period. This is either quarterly or yearly, depending on your preferred time frame.

At the end of any given period, you will want to review your cash flow statement. It's helpful for you, as the business owner, to see where your money is going and for getting a look at the trends with your business activities. It is also important to look ahead to know that you'll have the necessary funds in your account to meet upcoming obligations and money due to other vendors or banks.

Properly projecting your cash flow will help you determine what actions to take. Actions can include where to make cutbacks or if you'll be able to purchase new equipment if necessary. You will not know what actions to take if you aren't keeping track of your cash flow. This is an integral part of operating a business and is one of the fundamental parts of the accounting process in general.

Chapter 7

$------ \text{❧❦❦❧} ------$

How to Budget Your Business Finances

Budgeting properly is an important part of accounting. As the business owner, you'll want to make sure you are properly forecasting finances for the future and a rather large part of that is budgeting. This is also important because it helps you determine whether or not you are able to grow your business, buy new equipment, give raises to employees or even hire employees, or fund operations in general. This chapter will go over the six most common steps to take to properly budget your new business.

The Importance of Budgets

Before we go over the six steps to maintaining a budget, let's talk about why budgeting is so crucial to your business. A common mistake new business owners make is mishandling their finances. It doesn't mean they are not smart or unwise, but extra care needs to be taken with business finances. In life, we often make mistakes with money. We learn from it and move on. In business, there is so much more at stake. It's easy to look at the first couple of month's earnings and if they are much more than you expected, you get excited and start looking at ways to expand or purchase new equipment. This can put you in a bad position financially if the circumstances change.

Budgets also help minimize risk before expanding, signing leases, or investing in new equipment or machinery. Budgets can be used for a variety of things, including:

- Determining the funds needed for labor and materials

- Determining the costs of operating your business

- Estimating necessary startup costs

- Estimating what you can expect to earn

There are several components to budgeting, but a budget should always include your revenue, cost, and probably the most important components which are profit and cash flow. This is what will help you determine whether or not you have enough money left over to put into some kind of emergency fund or purchase new equipment. The budget should be calculated yearly and within that year, divvied up into twelve months. You'll leave a blank column on the sheet next to your estimated budget and at the end of each month, fill in your actual budget.

Now that we've covered the basics of budgeting, let's look at those six steps for keeping a budget for your small business.

1. **Check industry standards.** While all businesses differ in some way, there are also some common similarities. Do some research and check out the local library for industry specific information. Speak with other small business owners both inside and outside your niche and check the IRS website for an idea as to

what percentage of revenue can go back toward cost groupings. In this respect, you'll only need to research an average of these. Because small businesses are more susceptible to downturns in the industry, searching for specifics will prove tedious.

2. **Make a spreadsheet specific to your budget.** You will have several different sheets for cash flow, income statements and so on. You'll also want one dedicated to your budget. It's a good idea to have this prior to opening your business for the purposes of estimating total dollar amounts that will be allocated to your overall cost of raw materials. Your spreadsheet can also include budgetary items like rent, insurance and taxes.

3. **Factor in some slack.** Always remember that you are working with estimates and you'll want to make sure you have some reserve for anything unexpected that may come up. Not only do you want to plan for the unexpected, it's wise to prepare for expansion and paying new employees.

4. **Always be prepared to cut costs.** Sometimes, things get tight and you'll need to know where you can cut costs to pay an unexpected bill, capitalize on an opportunity, or advertise. In this instance, it is best to look at things that can be controlled on a larger scale. You can also wait to make any purchases until you begin a new billing cycle. Additionally, take advantage of any payment terms offered by suppliers and creditors.

5. **Review the business regularly**. Some businesses look at budgets on a yearly basis. Smaller, new businesses should make it a habit to keep an eye on budgets monthly or at the very least, quarterly. However, many small businesses make it a habit to look ahead a month at a time so they can better prepare themselves and keep close track of their finances.

6. **Shop around for suppliers and services**. This is a great way to save money and budget. Even if you have suppliers you've worked with for a while, it doesn't hurt to shop around and see if there are ways you can save money. If you've done business with a contractor for a while, they might be willing to match the price of a competitor to keep your business. There is absolutely nothing wrong with trying to find ways to save money and any other business owner will understand, even if they are unable to match the price. This is something that should be done at regular intervals. Once a year is sufficient for most industries. However, if you find you are struggling at any certain period, that would also be a good time to start to look at places you can make cutbacks. Shopping around for suppliers who will provide you with the things you need at a cheaper cost is the best place to start.

The bottom line is that budgeting for your business needs is a crucial part of owning and operating a business. The basic goal is to make sure you are earning enough money to keep the business going. Beyond that, you want to have enough money to compete with other businesses in your niche, grow your business and have a solid contingency fund. Not only that, if we are looking to the future and you would like to retire someday, you will want to prove that your business has been overall successful over the years. Potential buyers will pour over your books because they want to know that the business they might purchase will continue to earn them money just as it did for you while you were operating the company.

Chapter 8

— — — — — ❧❦❧ — — — — —

Tips to Keep on Track with Accounting

Accounting can be a dreaded task, especially if you are a new business owner. There are many things to keep on top of. Proper money management is one of the most crucial, however, and in this book we've covered several components of small business accounting. We will conclude with nine tips that will get and keep your small business accounting in order.

As we've discussed and as you've probably noticed, there are so many details associated with running your business. Making sure you have a good handle on the accounting basics from the beginning will be a key part of your company's success. Keeping track of revenue, costs, and expenses from the get go will ensure you don't drown in paperwork later on. Accounting is a necessary chore in business. *All business.* It helps you manage your day to day operations and will help keep you moving towards your long-term goals. It'll help you grow your business and raise revenue. The benefits of keeping your accounting in order far outweigh the tedious nature of performing the task itself.

1. **Separate personal and business expenses.** This sounds simple enough, but sometimes the lines get blurry and the two can get mixed in with one another. One of the best things you can do is get a separate bank account for your business. This includes separate checks and credit cards. Make sure to keep your receipts so that when it comes time to file taxes, you'll be able to deduct those items you used for your business. Another helpful tip here is to complete a monthly bank reconciliation for your business account. Take the time to do this once a month and you'll find that not only will it get easier as time goes on, but you'll also have all of that information readily available when it comes time to file those pesky taxes.

2. **Track every last one of your expenses.** This also sounds self-explanatory, right? You might think that tossing a receipt for a seemingly meaningless transaction won't hurt. In the long run, however, it just might. Save all of your receipts because when you own your own business, every deduction you can make does help. Along those lines, categorize and label all of your expenses. Track your cash flow so that you don't miss those tax write-offs. All of those deductions can add up quickly and will save you money in the long run. Also, if you aren't keeping close track of those expenses, you might find you are losing money. Use your business credit card for anything related to business needs. If for some reason you use cash or check, make sure you have a digital receipt filed.

3. **Accurately record deposits.** This is one of the areas your monthly bank reconciliation will come in handy. If you do happen to miss a deposit, you'll catch it on the monthly reconciliation. Revenue from sales, loans and other cash transactions are easy to lose track of, which can lead to your paying unnecessary taxes on those items. There are several software accounting programs you can use that will help you keep track of your deposits. If you choose to do this on your own, Excel is a great program to use.

4. **Understand and know when it 'pays to pay'.** If you feel overwhelmed, it could be helpful to hire an accountant, even if it is only for a few hours a week. Professional accountants are able to accurately track all of your records. It may cost a little bit of money, but it will save you some sanity. They are able to keep your records completely up to date and in proper order. Not to mention a professional is more likely to know about loopholes, potential fees or even some extra tax deductions for which you may be eligible. If you choose not to hire a professional, it helps to know accounting terms. Take some time to learn them so when you are researching things online, you'll have a better understanding of what you are looking at or looking for.

5. **Dedicate adequate time to update your books.** This is an incredibly important thing to remember. Do whatever is necessary to make sure you have the time to update your books! In the beginning, it might seem overwhelming, but consider setting aside some time each week to look at the books. That way, you are not letting the paperwork pile up and you are less likely to lose receipts or other important receivables.

Remember, this is a necessary part of running your own business.

6. **Keep tabs on your labor costs.** Payroll to employees and yourself is probably going to be your biggest expense. Make sure you are keeping track of overtime and other benefits to ensure that you are not over paying or under paying your employees. Or yourself! As the owner, you won't want to miss out on that paycheck. It's one of the reasons you went into business for yourself, right?

7. **Expect the unexpected and prepare for major expenses.** Over time, you'll need to be prepared for things like upgrading your computers and the systems that run on them, replacing equipment, and having enough money to cover your tax liability every year. Sometimes, you can be caught off guard by much larger, capital expenses, which unfortunately can come during your slowest months. It is best to plan ahead and have some extra money set aside just in case.

8. **Maintain your inventory records.** Keep close track of the dates you purchased your stock items and avoid misplacing them. Have a system in place that tracks where the item is stored so you know exactly where to look for it when the time comes. It helps to put your inventory into certain slots and to number it in a manner that will be easy for you to find. Within your inventory system, you'll want to have all purchase prices, sale prices and the date the inventory was sold.

9. **Follow-up on all receivables and invoices.** This can be tough. Just because you billed a customer does not mean they are going to immediately pay you. It is a good idea to have a system in place that lets you know when an invoice has not been paid. Whether you use a paper system or electronic, keeping track of who owes you what and when is an important part of the accounting process. Accepting online payments is also helpful. In instances where a customer is not paying on time, you will need to follow-up with them until they have sent in their payment. It is another not so fun part of accounting, but is entirely necessary. You want to get paid for the services or products you provided. That is part of being in business.

These nine tips are things for you to keep in mind while performing your accounting duties. Should you choose to keep the books on your own and not hire an accountant, keeping clean, accurate records will definitely minimize some of the stress associated with accounting!

Chapter 9

———— ❧❦❧ ————

Financial Ratios

Financial ratios are a great way to get a snapshot of your businesses performance, and also to compare it to similar businesses and previous time periods.

There are a range of different financial ratios that you can use to measure everything from liquidity, all the way to the earnings per share. The financial ratios of a business give a great look into how a company is performing, how durable it is, and what it might be worth.

As a small business, there are a handful of financial ratios that you should be using regularly. This chapter will cover these simple ratios that you must know, as well as a few others that you may or may not use, depending on the size and type of your business.

Current Ratio

This is one of the primary financial ratios that you will be using on a regular basis. This measures liquidity, and the ability a company has to pay current liabilities with current assets only.

Current Ratio = Total Current Assets/Total Current Liabilities

A 1:1 ratio is not where you want to be, because that means that you only have enough current assets to pay your current liabilities, and then will have nothing left over. This is not a very liquid position to hold, as it will leave you without any cash, and waiting on receivables.

A better ratio would be 2:1 as there, you have twice the ability to pay your current liabilities. For service based-businesses, this is a solid ratio to have, as the main expenses are salary and rent.

A ratio of 3:1 or higher may mean that you are too cash heavy. This isn't really an issue, but it does mean that you may not be making the best use of your cash, and could be reinvesting it further into growth.

It's important to understand and use this ratio often in order to ensure that you aren't strapped for cash in your business, and left waiting on receivables to be paid.

Gross Profit Ratio

The gross profit ratio shows the ability of a company to produce and sell products or offer a service, in a cost effective manner.

Gross Profit Ratio = Gross Profit/Sales

This formula will give you a look at the margin on each sale. For example, if a company did $20,000 in sales of a product, and the COGS (cost of goods sold) for those products was $10,000, that leaves us with $10,000 in gross profit. $10,000/$20,000 = 0.5:1 or 50%

That means that for every $1 of sales, the company makes a gross profit of $0.50.

This can be used in both service based, and product based businesses, though the ratios will vary quite a lot.

The important thing to take away from it is that there should be enough gross margin left to pay for the company's expenses, so they can make a net profit overall. This ratio can be used to see if changes in your business are improving margins, if some products are unprofitable, and what processes in your business might need improving.

Net Profit Ratio

The net profit ratio shows how much net profit is derived from every dollar of sales. Even though your business might have great gross margins, the net margins might tell a different story.

Net Profit Ratio = Net Profit/Net Sales

To turn this into a % figure, you simply multiply the result by 100.

The figures used for this calculation should be after tax numbers. This gives you an idea of the profitability of your business overall. While the gross profit ratio looks at the cost of producing a particular product, this calculation adds in the additional expenses involved with running a business such as staff, rent, utilities, etc. This ratio will give you an indication as to whether your expenses are too high, and will show you how changes you make to your business are effecting the overall profitability

Accounts Receivable Turnover Ratio

This ratio is used by businesses who invoice their clients rather than taking cash upon the sale. It measures your ability to collect payment from your credit customers. The higher ratio, the faster your collections are occurring. But be aware, if they are too quick, you may be deterring some customers. On the other hand, if your ratio is low, you might be short of cash in your business, and need to speed up the rate at which you are collecting payment. This is a good ratio to check regularly to see how your efficiency at collecting payments changes.

Accounts Receivable Turnover = Net Credit Sales/Average Accounts Receivable

Your average accounts receivable is an average of your last 2 years of receivables, divided by 2.

Days Sales Outstanding

This calculation expands on the previous one to show you the average amount of days it will take a customer on credit terms to pay you. If you have credit terms of 30 days, and on average customers are paying you after 45 days, that shows that you are doing a poor job of collecting payments on time.

Days Sales Outstanding = 365/Accounts Receivable Turnover Ratio

Quick Ratio

The quick ratio is very similar to the current ratio, but it gives a more conservative figure as to how liquid your business is.

Quick Ratio = Cash & Equivalents + Short Term Investments + Accounts Receivable/Current Liabilities

All of the current assets in this formula are easily converted to cash, whereas the current ratio includes some short-term assets that may be more difficult to liquidate, such as inventory.

It can be a good idea to calculate both the current and quick ratios for your business on a regular basis. This will help in ensuring that you don't run out of cash, and can remain liquid enough to be able to meet all of your current liabilities on short notice.

Profit Per Square Foot

This formula isn't used too often, but is a great indicator as to how well you are using your space.

Profit Per Square Foot = Net Profit (before tax)/Square Feet of Business Space

If you are expanding your business space to accommodate more staff, you have to ensure that these staff are contributing to the bottom line enough to justify the increase in rent for a larger location. This is where outsourcing some functions of your business may be a more logical choice.

Profit Per Head

Similar to profit per square foot, here you are calculating how much profit is derived from each staff member on average.

This can be used to measure the average value of sales staff, and to evaluate any individual's performance against the mean. When you make a new hire, you need to consider how much that person will contribute to your bottom line.

Profit Per Head = Net Profit (before tax)/Number of Full-Time Staff

Inventory Turnover Ratio

This is a measure of how frequently you are able to turn your inventory into sales. It gives you insight as to which products are selling well, and if you are managing inventory efficiently.

Inventory Turnover Ratio = Cost of Goods Sold/Average Inventory

Example:

COGS = $1750

Average Inventory = $1500

$1750/$1500 = 1.16

The greater the inventory turnover ratio, the more frequently the inventory is being converted to cash.

Debt to Worth Ratio

This ratio shows how dependent you are upon borrowed funds, compared to your own funding.

Debt to Worth Ratio = Total Liabilities/Net Worth

If your debt to worth ratio is greater than 1, then your business has more capital from lenders than from yourself. If you're looking for additional financing, a bank might see that as a risk.

ROI

The ROI or return on investment is a simple calculation that should be done regularly on different areas of your business. It measures if an investment was profitable or not, and by how much.

ROI = Earnings – Initial Cost of Investment/Initial Cost of Investment

Example:

Earnings = $20,000

Cost of Investment = $7,500

20,000 – 7,500 = 12,500

12,500/7,500 = 1.67

The higher your ROI, the more profit your investments are producing.

Chapter 10

— — — — — ✤✤✤ — — — — —

Stockholder's Equity

Stockholder's equity (also referred to as shareholder's equity) is a core component of a balance sheet, and represents the corporation's total 'book value'.

It can also be viewed as the owner's residual claim on the business after all liabilities have been paid, or as the source (along with liabilities) of the company's assets.

Although on some balance sheets the stockholder's equity is simply represented as the one figure, it is actually comprised of several components. In a detailed balance sheet, all individual components should be listed, and it's important to understand all of them. This is mainly applicable to larger businesses, but is still valuable to learn if you are operating a small business currently.

The different components of stockholder's equity are:

Paid in Capital

This subsection represents the amounts that the corporation received when it issued shares of capital stock.

Retained Earnings

Retained earnings are the cumulative earnings of the corporation, minus the cumulative amounts of dividends declared.

Accumulated Other Comprehensive Income

This is the cumulative amount of income, or loss, that has not been included in the net income reported on the corporation's income statement.

Treasury Stock

This is the amount the corporation has spent to re-purchase, but not retire, its own stock.

Chapter 11

－－－－－ ❧❦❧ －－－－－

Cash VS. Accrual

There are two different accepted accounting methods that you might choose to use, and those are the cash method, and the accrual method. Both methods will be discussed and explained in this chapter.

The main difference between the cash basis and accrual basis accounting is the timing of when revenues and expenses are recorded. In modern day business, a lot of transactions occur on credit terms, and payment isn't delivered until a later date. This begs the questions 'When do I record the transaction? When the transaction occurs, or when payment is received?'

This choice comes down to whether you use cash basis accounting or accrual basis accounting.

Most small businesses will use the cash method, and it is also the most-preferred method for personal finances. When using the cash method, you only record revenues and expenses when the actual cash is received or withdrawn.

On the other hand, the accrual method records these transactions when revenue is earned or when expenses are incurred, even if the payment is at a later date. This method is more common with larger businesses who deal with credit terms on a more regular basis. The accrual method is the most commonly used method of accounting overall, though it really depends upon your business and its needs.

It's important to stick to one method of accounting in order to accurately record your business transactions. If you were to use both methods sporadically it would become a lot harder to measure performance and track your cash flow – making a shortage of cash a much more likely possibility.

As an example of how the methods differ, let's imagine that your business sold $5,000 worth of machinery, but the payment is not made until 1 week after the transaction officially occurred and all documents were signed.

Under the accrual accounting method, you would record the transaction on the day that it occurred and all documents were signed. On the other hand, with the cash method you would not record the transaction until 1 week later when you received the cash or check.

Under the accrual method, it can be at times difficult to determine when exactly to record the transaction. Officially, it shouldn't be recorded until the service is completed in full, or the complete product has been provided. Likewise, you don't record an expense until it has been fully delivered, or completed to the contract's specifications. So even if a service takes 2 weeks to be completed, under the accrual method you would not record the transaction until the end of the 2 weeks, unless the payment was made prior to its delivery or completion.

As a larger business, you must use the accrual method of accounting. Once your business reaches sales of more than $5-million per year, or stocks items to sell to the public and has gross receipts of over $1-million, you are required to use the accrual method.

If your business isn't legally required to use the accrual method, the choice is up to you. There are of course, pros and cons to each method.

The accrual method will give you a more accurate look at the ebbs and flows of your business, however it can leave you in the dark as to how much of a cash reserve you have at a given period of time.

The cash method makes it simple to track just how much cash on hand you have at any given time, though it can give a skewed picture of business performance. Under the cash method, one month may look extremely profitable, while another may look dismal – all depending upon when you have received payments and paid your creditors.

Another factor to consider is your tax obligations. Depending upon when you record the transactions, you will owe tax at different points in time. If you use the accrual method of accounting for transactions but don't receive payment for them until the next financial year, you will still owe the payment during the financial year that the transaction was recorded.

Overall, neither method gives a complete picture of financial performance over a short-term basis. It's important to look at long-term figures, and to have a cash-flow budget in place to get an accurate measure of business performance.

Chapter 12

–––––– ✤✤✤✤ ––––––

Depreciation

Under the GAAP (Generally Accepted Accounting Principles), there are several methods of depreciation that may be used. Depreciation is where you can claim the devaluation of assets over time, against the amount of tax that your business owes.

The official GAAP definition of depreciation is as follows:

'Depreciation is a systematic and rational process of distributing the cost of tangible assets over the life of assets.'

Depreciation Methods Based on Time

Straight Line Method

This method of calculating depreciation is done as follows:

Depreciation = (Cost – Residual Value) / Useful Life

Example: On April 1, 2011, a company purchased equipment at a value of $140,000. This equipment is estimated to have a useful life of 5 years. At the end of the 5th year, the salvage value (residual value) will be $20,000. The company recognizes depreciation to the nearest whole month.

Depreciation value for 2011 = ($140,000 - $20,000) x 1/5 x 9/12 = $18,000

Depreciation value for 2012 therefore = ($140,000 - $20,000) x 1/5 x 12/12 = $24,000

Declining Balance Depreciation Method

Using this method, you calculate the depreciation as follows:

Depreciation = Book Value x Depreciation Rate

Book Value = Cost – Accumulated Depreciation

Example: Using the same example as above, and assuming the equipment once again has a useful life of 5 years with a residual value of $20,000, the company chooses to recognize depreciation to the nearest month.

Depreciation for 2011 = $140,000 x 40% x 9/12 = $42,000

Depreciation for 2012 = ($140,000 - $42,000) x 40% x 12/12 = $39,200

Sum of the Year's Digits Depreciation Method

Here, where 'n' represents the number of years of useful life, depreciation is calculated as follows:

Depreciation Expense = (Cost – Salvage Value) x Fraction

Fraction for the first year = n / (1+2+3+...+n)

Fraction for the second year = (n-1) / (1+2+3+...+n)

Fraction for the third year = (n-2) / (1+2+3+...+n)

Fraction for the last year = 1 / (1+2+3+...+n)

Example: A company purchased an asset on January 1, 2011. The acquisition cost of the asset is $100,000 and the useful life of the asset is 5 years. The residual value of the asset at the end of useful life is $10,000.

Depreciation expense for 2011 = ($100,000 - $10,000) x 5/15 = $30,000

Depreciation expense for 2012 = ($100,000 - $10,000) x 4/15 = $24,000

Which Method to Use

The straight line method of calculating depreciation is the most commonly used method. It charges an equal amount of depreciation to each accounting period, and is the simplest to calculate. Though, the choice of which method you use is largely up to you. Your choice should depend upon which method is most suitable for your business, and the assets which you are calculating it for.

Chapter 13

———— ✦❧✦❧ ————

Inventory Accounting

Accounting for inventory can be a difficult thing to do, and there are several different methods for doing so.

The most commonly used accounting systems are the perpetual inventory system, and the periodic inventory system.

Perpetual

The perpetual system requires that accounting records show the amount of inventory on hand at all times. It holds a separate account in the subsidiary ledger for each good in stock, and is updated any time the inventory levels change.

Determining the COGS (cost of goods sold) requires taking inventory. The most common methods of valuating the inventory under a perpetual system are:

- First in, first out (FIFO)

- Last in, first out (LIFO)

- Highest in, first out (HIFO)

- Average Cost

These methods all produce different results because they are based upon differing assumptions.

With the FIFO method, you are basing the cost flow on the chronological order in which purchases are made. With LIFO on the other hand, you are basing the cost flow in a reverse chronological order. The average cost method produces a cost flow based on the average cost of goods.

The important thing here is to simply stick with one method of recording your inventory.

Periodic

In the periodic system, sales are recorded at the time they occur, but the inventory is not updated. A physical inventory count must be taken at the end of year to determine the cost of goods for that period.

Which Method to Choose?

The choice of which inventory management system you use (if you require one) is up to you. There are however, a few key differences to be aware of before making your decision.

To record purchases using the periodic system, you will debit the Purchases Account. Conversely, doing the same using the perpetual system you will debit the Merchandise Inventory account.

To record sales, the perpetual system requires an entry to debit the COGS and another to credit the Merchandise Inventory. By recording the COGS for each sale, the perpetual system alleviates the need for adjusting entries and calculating

COGS at the end of a financial period, which can be a big time-saver.

Chapter 14

————————— ❧❦•❦❧ —————————

Definitions of Accounting Terms

Accounting can be over-complicated at times by different acronyms and terms. This chapter is dedicated to defining the most common accounting terms that you'll come across.

Accounts Receivable (AR)

The amount of money owed by your customers after goods or services have been delivered.

Accounts Payable (AP)

The amount of money you owe creditors in return for the goods or services that they have delivered.

Current Assets (CA)

Current assets are assets that will be used within one year. Typically, this will include cash, inventory, and accounts receivable.

Fixed Assets (FA)

Fixed assets are assets that are long-term, and will likely provide benefits to a company for more than one year. Examples are a building, land, or machinery.

Balance Sheet (BS)

A financial report that summarizes a company's assets, liabilities, and owner's equity at a given time.

Capital (CAP)

A financial asset and its value, such as cash or goods. Working capital is calculated by subtracting current liabilities from current assets.

Cash Flow (CF)

The revenue or expense that is expected to be generated through business activities over a given period of time.

Certified Public Account (CPA)

A CPA is someone who has passed a CPA accounting exam and met the government-mandated work and educational requirements to be considered a CPA.

Cost of Goods Sold (COGS)

The direct expense involved in producing the goods sold by a company. This may include the raw materials, and amount of employee labor used for production.

Credit (CR)

An accounting entry when there is either a decrease in assets, or increase liabilities and equity on the balance sheet.

Debit (DR)

An accounting entry when there is either an increase in assets, or a decrease in liabilities on the balance sheet.

Expenses (Fixed, Variable, Accrued, Operation) = (FE, VE, AE, OE)

The fixed, variable, accrued, or day-to-day expenses that a business incurs through its operation.

Generally Accepted Accounting Principles (GAAP)

These are a set of rules and guidelines that were developed by the accounting industry for companies to follow when reporting financial data.

General Ledger (GL)

A complete record of the financial transactions of a company over its lifespan.

Liabilities (Current & Long-Term) = (CL & TL)

The debts and financial obligations of a company. Current liabilities are those due to be paid within one year, whereas long-term liabilities are typically payable over a longer period of time – such as a bank loan.

Net Income (NI)

The total net earnings of a company. This is calculated by subtracting all expenses from the total revenue.

Owner's Equity (OE)

This is typically explained as the percentage amount of ownership a person has in a company. To calculate as a dollar figure, it is the remaining figure after all liabilities are subtracted from all assets.

Present Value (PV)

The value of how much a future sum of money is worth today. The value of money will change over time due to inflation, so $100 today is not worth the same amount as $100 in 10-years time. Present value helps us to understand this.

Profit & Loss (P&L)

A financial statement that is used to summarize the performance of a company over a given period of time. It summarizes all revenues, costs, and expenses that a company incurs over a period of time.

Return on Investment (ROI)

A measurement of how much of a return that a company made from a particular investment. It is calculated by dividing the net profit by the cost of the investment. It is often presented as percentage figure.

Conclusion

— — — — — ❧❧❦❦❦ — — — — —

Thanks again for taking the time to read through this book!

You should now have a good understanding of accounting, and be ready to tackle the accounting of your own business!

If you enjoyed this book, please take the time to leave me a review on Amazon. I appreciate your honest feedback, and it really helps me to continue producing high quality books.